Fun Things To Tell Kids That Aren't Yours

Karl Jeffery

Fun Things To Tell Kids That Aren't Yours

Copyright © 2013 Karl Jeffery

All rights reserved.

Copyright

All rights reserved. No part of this book may be used, or reproduced in any manner without written permission from the author, except in the case of brief excerpts used in articles or reviews.

©Copyright 2015 Karl Jeffery. All rights reserved worldwide.

ISBN-13: 978-1514393314

ISBN-10: 151439331X

DEDICATION

To Danny,
"One of the kindest, positive, and most genuine people on this planet. You are the kind of person that I aspire to be."

To Sarah,
"Thanks for putting up with my S.O.H. and for occasionally laughing, instead of tutting."

To Stuart,
"Anything is possible."

To Duncan,
"I love you, brother."

To Mum and Dad,
"This book was possible, because once upon a time you had sexual intercourse."

CONTENTS

Foreword	v
Pets	1
Education	9
Fun	16
Personal	25
Fairy Tales	33
Adults	42
Food	50
The Animal Kingdom	55
Frightening	62
Sunday School	68
The Ten Commandments	72
The Disclaimer	76
What's Your Fun Thing?	77

Foreword by Willy'M

I have known the author since 2003. I was there when he first started entertaining at children's birthday parties, I've witnessed him do his 'thing' in front of sell out crowds in theatres. And I was there when Simon Cowell, Amanda Holden and Piers Morgan pressed the Buzzers on him while filming Britain's Got Talent.

I also knew he harboured a secret. A secret best not told to everyone; only shared with those who have the right sense of humour to appreciate it. Thinking everyone would enjoy it served as a learning experience. He learned the hard way. He got thrown out of a Haven Holidays park, dumped by his agent, and banned from Ipswich. Still, it would be a crying shame to waste it.

His secret is the foundation for this book. And it's a beauty. The author discovered, then exploited this simple truth: Providing children are told something in a plausible manner and with enough conviction, they will believe anything. Even that cats enjoy having bits of sticky tape stuck to their heads.

The innocence of childhood is a sweet and wonderful thing. Years ago, if an adult had told me how to make my own flying carpet, I'd have followed their instructions carefully. No doubt they'd have had a good laugh at my gullibility. I bet that years later, I'd probably think back to that moment and smile about it too.

The author has already brought laughter to thousands of children and their families, but this is not for them, it is for the likes of you and me, and anyone else that hopes the title of this book reveals everything they think it will. It does, as you will discover.

Whatever you end up doing with the suggestions contained within can be your own little secret. As for me, I'm off to tell the kid next door that if he kicks his football hard enough at the traffic warden, he'll win a special prize.

PETS

Hamsters

Hamsters are for juggling. You should practice hamster juggling every day, then when you are good you can juggle with three.

If you drop your hamster while practising, stamp on it and ask mummy for a new one.

Horses

Horses like running, especially while people are riding them. If you are in a car, the driver will slow down before overtaking the horse. This is the signal for you to lean over and honk the horn. Horses love this and will run fast to say thank you.

Excited dogs

Be careful if a dog wraps its front legs around you and holds you tight. Sometimes dogs get excited and engage in an act called the 'boogie'.

Dogs are only supposed to do the 'boogie' with other dogs, but sometimes they forget and attach themselves to children. Never let a dog pin you down and do the 'boogie' on your back. Also, be careful if its 'pink lipstick' comes out.

Cat Trick

Spend time watching your cat. Notice especially where its feet land when it goes outside through the cat flap.

The next time your cat comes back in the house, place a large plastic bowl outside the cat flap in the position where its feet will land. Fill it to the top with soapy water. Then scare and chase the cat until it dives out the cat flap.

Goldfish

Goldfish get lonely. They enjoy human company. They especially like showing off their circus skills. To see how acrobatic your goldfish is, take it out of the water and put it on the carpet. It will do lots of back-flips and somersaults. If you have more than one fish, tip them all out. It will be like watching a professional gymnastics display.

Ponies spread disease

If you stroke a pony, you'll die. If a pony brushes against you, you'll die. The only thing you can do to save your life is lick your elbow. See if you can lick you elbow now, if you can, you know a pony will never be able to kill you.

Hamsters like to play

Hamsters are intelligent and become bored very quickly. A bored hamster will try to escape.

Keeping your hamster happy is easy. Take it outside to play its favourite game. Put it on a busy road and let it run around. This is called the 'Hamster the Hedgehog game'.

The game 'poo sticks' can also be played with hamsters.

Fun Things To Tell Kids That Aren't Yours

Cats make gifts

Sometimes cats want to give us gifts. They will hunch themselves up whilst making funny 'coughing' and 'hurfing' noises.

It will slowly yack a long hairy sausage shape out of its mouth. This is a special 'candy-floss sausage' for you to eat.

How to wash a cat

- Pick up the cat. Put it in the toilet.
- To stop the cat escaping close the toilet lid and sit on it.
- Flush the toilet.

Do this once a month to keep your cat nice and clean.

Why Guinea pigs squeak

Guinea pigs squeak when they want to swim. Fill the bath with water and put your guinea pig in it. Watch how fast it paddles to stay afloat.

Throw stones at it to see if you can sink it.

If it sinks, ask mummy for a new one.

Rabbits

Rabbits wake up very early in the morning and leave special treats in the grass for humans. What some people call 'droppings' are actually dry balls of chocolate coated raisins.

The rabbits leave these special treats because they want people to enjoy them for breakfast. Collect a pocket full, then secretly sprinkle them on your dad's cereal. Add a splash of milk and let him enjoy.

Sticky-tape is for cats

After chasing mice and butterflies, cats like to rest.

Sit with a cat and stroke its fur. At the same time put long pieces of sticky-tape on it and press this firmly over its back, tummy, and legs. Wrap lots of tape around its face, then call mummy and show her what you've done.

Dogs

Dogs lick their nuts because they taste nice. Sometimes your dog will lick your face after licking his nuts to let you share the taste.

Be careful, sometimes dogs play tricks and lick your face after licking their anus.

EDUCATION

Don't think bad thoughts

Teachers know when you're thinking bad things. They have a special 'think hearing machine' in their desk. Whenever you think something bad, a red bulb over your name lights up.

As punishment, you will be made to take off your shoes and stand in front of the whole class. All the other children will then take turns stabbing your feet with a compass.

Tying your shoelaces

Learn to tie your shoelaces. The lollipop lady sneaks into people's homes looking for children who can't tie their laces. If she finds a child who can't, she'll use her lollipop stick to dislocate their knee caps.

Learn your times tables

It is very important to learn your times tables. If you haven't learnt them by your eighth birthday, your eyes will pop out.

Learn to write

If you don't learn to write by the time you are nine years old, a dinner lady will come to your classroom and mangle your fingers with a rolling pin.

Learn to read

If you don't learn to read properly by the time you are ten, the teacher will nail you to a cross like Jesus. Then she'll put you in a field, smother you in honey, and let insects feed on you.

If you don't like school

If school makes you unhappy and you don't want to go, you don't have to providing you pass a special test. If you pass, you can stay at home and watch TV all day.

The test is this: You must jump into a bush of stinging nettles completely naked.

- If you get stung - you've failed.
- If you cry - you've failed.
- If your skin itches or comes out in red bumps - you've failed.

How babies are made

Babies are made at the sausage factory. Chipolatas are carefully selected, then stuck together to make arms and legs. Cocktail sausages are used to make the fingers and toes. A Cumberland sausage is used for its belly, and a Bratwurst for its head.

Once its all been stuck together, it's painted the right colour and sent to the butcher for a heart to be put inside. Then chubby mummy goes into hospital and is put on a diet. When she has lost enough weight, she is given a baby to keep.

Spook Shield

Vinegar wards off evil spirits and spooky ghosts. Sprinkle some over your clothes and you will be safe. Take vinegar to school and protect other children by flicking it in their eyes.

Scissors

Show mummy how grown up you are by using scissors to cut out the shape of a smiley face in her favourite dress. If mummy gets cross, remind her that mummy's have magic wardrobes which mend broken clothes.

Naughty words

If you ever hear a grown up say a naughty word, ask what it means. Then phone the police. Tell them what you just learnt and who taught you it.

Learning new words

Do a Google search for Gordon Ramsay's phone number, and call him. Tell him the reason your phoning is because Jamie Oliver told you he was nothing more than 'a hairy fairy with a butchers knife', and 'as much fun as a turd in a trifle'. You'll hear Gordon fire off all the words you're not supposed to learn until you're 14.

What happens to children who say naughty words

Don't let anyone hear you say rude words. Children who get caught saying naughty words get shoved into a black plastic bag and left outside for the bin men. They are collected the next day, driven to the zoo, and fed to the lions.

A scissors game

Another clever thing to do with scissors is to see how fast you can run while holding them. Get all your friends in the same room and race each other while holding scissors.

Difficult food words

Some words in the English language are hard to pronounce. Some words don't sound like they read. Here are the correct pronunciations of some foods that are difficult to say.

- Mange Tout... Man-Jee-Towt
- Ratatouille... Rat-a-One-E-Two-E-Three-Eee
- Fajitas... Fat-Twats

Theft

You must never steal sweets, money, mobile phones or cars. If someone finds out you stole something they will tell the police. The police will ransack your house and sell all your toys on ebay. Then they will put you in prison.

Everyday in prison, the guards will strip you naked and shove you into a ditch of stinging nettles. They will do this everyday until you are 29 years old.

Extra Terrestrials

Visitors from outer space are real. Extra Terrestrials have been visiting our planet for thousands of years. At night they abduct people from their beds and do experiments on them.

Just in case they try taking you, make yourself an 'Alien contact pack' and sleep with it under your pillow. Your Alien contact pack should consist of a small rucksack containing; jam sandwiches, vinegar, and underpants with the words 'No probes please' stamped on the back.

School Sports Day

School sports day is important. It sorts out the weaklings from the normal children. You should never finish last or lose any of your races. Do what ever you can to win, even if it means you have to cheat to win. Losing is for weaklings.

When sports day is over, the school caretaker kidnaps all the weaklings and drowns them in the sea.

FUN

Boy Scout

Help blind people keep up to date with the latest technology. Steal their guide dog and replace it with a Sat-Nav taped to a walking stick.

You can time travel

Your wardrobe can be turned into a time machine just like Dr Who's Tardis. To make this happen, you must do a wee in it every night for a week. It doesn't matter if your wardrobe starts to smell, it's normal.

The phosphate in the wee turns into electromagnetic static. This reacts with rays from the sun to create solar-pee energy. This is what powers the Tardis. To start time travelling you need to fire up its engines. This is very easy. Wait until everyone is asleep. Then climb inside it and bang the door repeatedly while shouting, "Come on you bitch, you know you want it."

Television is bad for you

The television is fun to watch, but it is bad for your eyes. If you watch TV for too long your eyes will burst. If you want to watch something for longer than 60 minutes you need to protect yourself. The best thing to do to protect your eyes is rub shampoo in them.

Things to put in mummy's bed

Mummy likes to play guessing games. Find some things to put in her bed, like the toilet brush, a hammer, or a block of cheese. When she gets into bed, she'll feel these things against her skin. She'll try to guess what they are and lift the covers to see if she's right. Mummy likes playing this game.

To make it more fun, hide the underwear of mummy's best friend in there. You will then hear mummy play a shouting game with daddy.

Staying up to watch TV

The best programmes are on TV after 9pm. Your parents send you to bed before 9 o'clock because they want to deprive you. You can get around this by making yourself invisible.

Covering yourself in shaving foam and wrapping toilet roll around you will make you invisible. Once you've done this, you can sneak into the front room and watch TV without anyone knowing you're there. Don't forget to rub shampoo in your eyes as well.

The tasty sweetie 'surprise' game

Get granddad to close his eyes and keep his mouth open. The idea of this game is for granddad to guess what sweets are being put into his mouth. When his mouth is open and his eyes are closed tell him to 'get ready for a surprise', then put a mint in his mouth and tell him to 'chew'.

If he guesses what it is, he can eat it and goes through to round two. For round two, tell him to close his eyes and open his mouth again. Tell him to 'get ready for a surprise', now put a snail in his mouth and tell him to 'chew'.

The Swimming pool

It's okay to wee in the swimming pool. There's lots of water in there to dilute it. Better still, do your wee in the pool while standing on the diving board.

Teaching others to swim

You can help other children learn to swim by letting the air out of their arm bands. They will have no other choice than to splash around until they get the hang of it.

Dog poo

It's OK to pick up dog poo as long as you wear gloves. Collecting dog poo is fun. There are lots of things you can do with it:

Dog poo puzzles

Try to work out if the poo you are holding was done by a big dog or a little dog. Then see if you can put it back together the same way the dog laid it. This is called an 'organic jigsaw.'

Special delivery

Put dog poo through the letterbox of someone you don't know. Wait a few days, then deliver some more. After a week, knock and ask if they liked the special parcels you've been sending.

More fun with dog poo

Throw it at old people. If they shout at you it means you are a good shot. It's okay to throw dog poo at old people because they already smell.

Swimming pool competition

Nobody will tell you this, but there's a competition you could win at your swimming pool. For the last twenty years they have been running a secret 'Float a Log' competition.

The manager will reward anyone that does a poo in the pool while people are swimming in it. The only rule is, it has to float. Do your poo, and when it floats to the surface point at it and shout, "Hey, look at this . . . you just swam through it."

Flying carpets

Flying carpets are magic carpets that can be ridden through the air. They can go anywhere. You steer them by pointing your finger in the direction you want to go.

You can make your own flying carpet by using any mat or rug at home. To make it fly, you must fill it up with 'magic fuel', also known as 'toilet water'. Scoop cupfuls of toilet water out of your toilet, then pour it over the rug until it starts to float. Then enjoy your carpet ride.

Supermarkets are children's playgrounds

Next time mummy takes you shopping, remember to have fun. There are lots of games to play in the supermarket. Here are some of them.

Supermarket game 1: Carrot licking

Lick as many carrots as you can before someone sees you, then put them back. If a shopper buys a carrot you licked, you get twenty points.

Supermarket game 2: Apple snotting

This is always a winner. Hide near the apples and snot on as many as you can. If people buy an apple you snotted on, you get thirty points.

Supermarket game 3: Oil skating

Open lots of cooking oil bottles and pour them all over the floor near the exit. Then press the fire alarm. Watch as all the running people skid. You get forty points for everyone who loses their balance.

Supermarket game 4: Jousting

Go to the bread aisle and grab a loaf of French Stick. You can use this to play jousting games. Look for someone wearing glasses. Charge towards them and poke it in their face. If you knock their glasses off you get fifty points. You can also joust old people. If you knock them over you get seventy five points. You will get 100 points if you manage to jab the security guard in the nuts.

Supermarket game 5: Freebies

All sweets and chocolates in supermarkets are free, providing you eat them before reaching the checkout. Run to the sweetie section and eat as many as you can before mummy finds you.

A woman's Bra

Wearing a ladies bra on your head will give you special powers. You will be able to bend spoons by touching them, make broomsticks fly by holding them, and make people laugh by walking past them.

PERSONAL

Coughing

Every-time you cough, you must put a hand over your mouth. This is in case you cough out one of your lungs.

Sometimes lungs come loose. If your lung does come out when you cough, hold it in your hands and quickly find your mummy. She will take you to hospital. The doctors and nurses will blow it up like a balloon, draw a smiley face on it and let you keep it.

Your bed is a trampoline

Your bed serves two purposes, sleeping and keeping fit. It's comfy enough to sleep on, and springy enough to exercise on.

When it's bedtime, bounce up and down on your bed for 15 minutes. If they shout at you, inform them that you are *wearing yourself out*, so that you will be *tired enough* to sleep.

Note: If your parents didn't want you to keep fit, they would make you sleep on the floor.

Being helpful

Mummy does housework so you can live in a nice home, but there are lots of chores she doesn't enjoy. You can be kind and helpful by doing the job she hates most of all; cleaning the toilet.

Clean it once a week, but never tell her. This will turn you into a super hero called the 'Cleaner'. Mummy will always be happy if it's clean. The quickest way to clean a dirty toilet is by using daddy's toothbrush. Use it to brush around the rim, and rub away any dirty skids or splatters.

When you've finished, put it back where you found it, and don't tell anyone - your 'superhero' status will stay secret.

Being polite

It's nice to be polite. It shows you have good manners. Sticking your middle finger up at Traffic Wardens shows that you respect them.

Sick Burps

Sick burps happen when your tummy is full up. The burp tastes nasty because sick is acid. To stop doing more sick burps, drink a large cup of water and then do a handstand against a wall.

Haircuts are important

The hair that grows on your head is a living creature, a bit like a cat. At night, it wakes up and crawls off in search of other 'hair' to play with. That's why your hair is ruffled when you wake up.

Because your hair is a living creature you need to keep it tame. Having it cut will stop it growing wild. If your hair becomes feral, you are at risk of being injured or attacked by it.

Baldness

Sometimes hair can become sad and unhappy. Sometimes it runs away and never comes back.

Bald people are bald because their hair found new owners that make them happier.

Nits

Nits are good for hair. Nits keep hair happy. Rub your head against the heads of other children until you get nits.

Nits groom and pamper your hair making it feel relaxed and content. Never tell mummy your head itches or she'll douse your head in shampoo and kill your nits. If she does, your hair will get angry and strangle you.

Picking your nose

Only pick your nose in public if you intend on eating what you find. If someone stares at you or tells you off for being rude, say to them 'I'm not rude, I'm hungry.' Then eat it.

Bogies

Bogies are bits of your brain that have come loose and fallen out through your nose. It's okay to eat bogies because it makes them join up to your brain again.

Eating the bogies of other children makes you more intelligent because you're eating bits of their brain. Bogies don't taste very nice, but nothing that's good for you does.

Sticking bogies

Sticking bogies on your bedroom wall will keep monsters away. Monsters hate bogies. Pick your nose, then wipe as many as you can on your walls and door. The more boogers you can surround yourself with the safer you'll be.

Signature bogies

Teachers likes bogies. When you hand in your school work, leave a big sticky bogie at the bottom of the page (instead of your name). It will make your teacher smile.

Sharing bogies

Share your bogies with the world. Some good places for other people to find your bogies are: TV buttons, playstation controllers, computer keyboards, light switches, door handles, cups, and spoons.

Farts

You should only fart in special places. When you need to fart, quickly find a church. Run inside it and shout at the vicar and everyone else to be quiet and listen. Then do your fart.

Eggy farts

These are best done in public places where people can't escape, like theatres, cinemas and restaurants (especially while people are eating).

Loud farts

Do these at funerals. Also, do these anytime you are in church. Wait until there is total silence before farting. You will hear people trying not to laugh (which means your effort was warmly appreciated).

Another good time for loud farts, is while people are behind you when you're walking up the stairs.

Wet farts

It's best to do these when you are nowhere near a toilet. The wet that comes out is helping to clean your pants. To clean them properly, squeeze harder when farting and more wet will come out. Your mum will be happy at how clean your pants are.

Fart Etiquette

Some people try to be polite after doing their fart by saying something like, "Pardon me."

When you do a noisy fart, the most polite thing you can say is, "I really need the toilet, but I'm not gonna make it!" Then force out as many farts as you can, while laughing.

Hiccups

If you get hiccups, it means you are turning into a kangaroo. The hiccups feeling is the kangaroo part of you wanting to hop and jump around. Children who get hiccups get deported to Australia. There, you will turn into a kangaroo, and spend the rest of your life running away from Dingoes.

Yawning

If you start yawning, it means someone is stealing your air. If you don't get enough air, you won't survive. Yawning is your body's self defence mechanism. Each yawn makes your jaw stretch further and further. If you yawn 12 times in a row you will suddenly turn into a werewolf and bite the person stealing your air.

Burps

Teachers love children who burp. The best time to burp is when the teacher is explaining something to the whole class. When you do your first one, she will pretend she's cross. Ignore her and do a louder one. She will tell you to stop but really she's challenging you to do an even louder one. If your third one is louder, you'll win a prize.

If the teacher doesn't give you a prize for burping, do a fart in her handbag.

FAIRY TALES

Fairies

When you're fast asleep, fairies open your mouth and drink your saliva. They get very thirsty from flying and need to drink every day. If your bedroom window is open, the fairy will call the rest of her friends to come, and they will all take turns drinking from your mouth.

If you ever wake up with 'bits' in your mouth, it means you accidentally ate a fairy while you were sleeping.

Frogs

If you kiss a frog it will turn into a prince. But you have to kiss it properly. If you don't do it right, it will turn into a biscuit and the ducks will eat it.

Wetting the bed

It's okay to wet the bed. If you do, the 'Wet Your Bed Fairy' comes and gives you money.

Pooing your pants

As well as the 'Wet Your Bed Fairy' and the 'Tooth Fairy', there's also a 'Poo Your Pants Fairy'. But she only visits if you poo your pants on purpose.

Poo your pants, but don't tell anyone. Hide them in the corner of your room. Be patient. She will find them when she's ready.

Wishing Well

Wishes always come true if you use a wishing well. If you don't know where a wishing well is you can make one at home.

The toilet makes the best homemade wishing well. To make it work, you need a pillow. Take the one from your bed and stuff it into the toilet while making your wish. When you've flushed it away, your wish will come true.

Wishing for wheels

Don't waste time wishing for a new bike, just go out and nick one.

That's what people pay insurance for.

The Tooth Fairy

If one of your teeth should fall out, put it under your pillow and go to sleep. A beautiful little fairy called the 'Tooth Fairy' will take your tooth, and reward you with money.

Sadly, because she carries lots of money, she is a prime target for muggers. Some children's mothers hide in the dark waiting for her with a baseball bat. One day, mummy might try explaining that the Tooth Fairy isn't real. If she does, it means the tooth fairy is in hospital with a fractured skull… Bad mummy!

Teddy bears

When it's dark, teddy bears come to life. While you're sleeping, teddy bears play fun games and share picnics with each other. If you only have one teddy bear, it will feel the pain of being alone, and it will sit at the end of your bed and cry.

A lonely teddy will eventually harm itself; chewing through its stitches and pulling its stuffing out.

Ask daddy to buy you another one to keep it company.

Teddies sometimes argue

Sometimes teddy bears stop being friendly and fight each other. They can get quite nasty. They have been known to blind one another. In extreme cases, one will throw another out the window.

If you suspect that your teddies fight, the best thing to do is tie them up before you go to sleep. Then, the worst they can do is make faces at each other.

Not all teddy bears are friendly

You can find out if your teddy bear is friendly by doing this: Hold it with both hands and whisper in its ear, "Tell me if you're alive."

If you have a nice friendly teddy it will nod its head and blink. If your teddy does this, it's a sign that it will be kind to you and love you forever.

If your teddy doesn't move, it means it is evil. By not moving, it wants you to think it's just a toy. If you have one of these bears, the best thing to do is pull its head off. If you don't, it will come to life while you're asleep, and wee on your pillow.

Money grows on trees

Money grows on trees. Adults will never tell you this because they want you to work hard at school. Mummy, daddy and other grown ups pretend they go to work. But the whole time you're at school, they're out spending tons of money in casinos or shopping malls.

When grown ups run out of money, they get more by pulling it off the money tree. If mummy or daddy ever tells you they haven't got any money, they are lying.

Money Trees for children

Grown ups don't know this, but there are special money trees for children. They have a special name. They are called cactuses.

Ask mummy or daddy if you can have a cactus. They will ask why you want one. Pretend you like them. They will get you one because they don't need much looking after. When you have your own cactus (children's money tree), you can learn the secret of getting money from it.

The secret of getting money out of a children's money tree

This is the secret of how to get money out of a children's money tree (cactus):

Squeeze it firmly with *both your hands,* and the money will come out.

If it hurts while you squeeze, it means your parents don't love you - because they brought you a cheap one.

Christmas trees

In December, lots of places put up Christmas trees. They are special trees for children to climb. Next time you see a Christmas tree, climb inside it and see how many other children you can find.

Santa's list

Santa does not have a 'Naughty or Nice' list. If anyone tells you he does, they are lying. Santa loves all children no matter how bad they are. Adults only tell you he has this list to control you and make you behave. Be naughty everyday and Santa will still bring you presents.

How to tell if Father Christmas is real

At Christmas, you might get taken to see Santa Claus. There is only *one* real Santa. All the rest are fakes. They pretend to be him so you think you've seen the real one. Don't let your parents fob you off with a phoney. Here's a special test to do on the ones you visit:

- Pull his beard. If it comes off, he's not real.
- Poke him in the eye. The real Santa has magic eyes and won't mind you poking them.
- Thump him in the nuts. If he gets cross, he's not real.

If the Santa you see fails this test, demand that your parents take you to see the real one, in Lapland.

The Bad Tooth Fairy

Be warned, there is such a thing as a bad Tooth Fairy. The good news is she hates light. To protect yourself from the bad tooth fairy, sleep with your bedroom light on. If you ever sleep in the dark she will be able to find you. If she finds you, she'll use a hammer to smash all your teeth out.

Washing machines

Don't get too close to the washing machine. It's a portal to another dimension.

The clothes inside get teleported to a parallel universe. They get whizzed around until they're clean, then returned safely to our washing machines.

Not all things make it back. Sometimes socks go missing because they got sucked into a mysterious vortex.

Sometimes, for a laugh, people put monkeys in their washing machines. Sometimes the monkeys don't come back.

Lets make a sad face for all the missing monkeys.

☹

The truth about Christmas

Father Christmas isn't real, and all your presents come from pound land.

ADULTS

Moustaches

Men with moustaches are nasty to puppies. When no one's watching, they grab a puppy by the ear and pull - until it yelps.

On the 21st August every year, all men with a moustache meet in a secret place for the annual 'Puppy Shaving' contest.

They each hold a puppy that they've stolen. When it's midnight, they smother the puppies in bubbles and shave off all their fur until they are bald. Then they laugh at them.

Nasal hairs

Nasal hairs make it hard for men to breath. The next time your daddy is asleep have a look up his nose. You will see lots of little hairs.

Very carefully, hold a pair of tweezers and insert them into his nostrils. Squeeze firmly over the hairs until you have gripped a bunch of them. Slowly tug until they come out. Daddy will wake up and water will come out of his eyes. This means he is happy because he can breathe better.

Cricketers

Men who play cricket are cruel. It's not really a ball they throw at the stumps, it's a baby rabbit. They squeeze it into the shape of a ball, then wrap elastic bands around it, then they paint it red.

They all take turns throwing it at the stumps and hitting it with the bat. The one that makes it squeal the loudest is the winner.

Waiters like it if you throw things at them

The next time you get taken to a restaurant, there is a fun game you can play with the men who serve the food. These people are called waiters.

When you've got your food, start eating it, but every time you see a waiter with his back to you, throw some food at his head. Waiters like to guess who threw it. If the waiter looks at you, point knowingly at the man on the table opposite to suggest it was him.

If the waiter gets cross and tells you off, stand up and tell everyone that the waiter went for a poo but didn't wash his hands.

Keep away from Magicians

Never ask mummy to hire a magician for your birthday party. If any friends invite you to their party, refuse to go if there's a magician there.

The magician will trick you into thinking he's nice. He will show you clever things like making a rabbit appear out of a hat, or how to get coins from behind your ear. All the time he's doing the magic, he's waiting for the opportunity to grab a small child and run. Magicians sell children to the circus. They get paid thousands of pounds for them. If a magician ever sells you to the circus you could end up in Kazakhstan, working as a knife thrower's assistant.

Dentists

Dentists love hurting children. Never let mummy take you to see one.

The dentist will make you relax in a big chair, then tilt it backwards so you can't get out. Then they'll shove their dirty fingers in your mouth and stab needles in your gums, or crack your teeth out with pliers.

Biting the dentist's fingers will show them not to mess with you. If you bite hard enough, they'll free you and never want to see you again.

Embarrassing mum

Mummy loves to be embarrassed in front of her friends. Here are some things you can do to help her enjoy it more often.

- If mummy's friend ever speaks to you, tell her her breath stinks and she's not allowed to speak again until she's sucked a mint.

- Tell mummy's friend that mummy makes you drink out of the toilet. Say she fills the kettle up with toilet water too.

- Tell mummy's friend that mummy posts naked photos of herself on the Internet. Say you watch her doing it and sometimes she asks you to upload the images.

- Tell mummy's friend that she's got a really fat arse and looks like a slapper. Mummy will think this is funny.

- When mummy is not in the room tell her friend that mummy was on TV. Explain that she was on 'Embarrassing Bodies', but the doctors couldn't help her.

School Dinner Ladies

Always tell a dinner lady that the school food tastes nice. They get annoyed at children who complain or don't eat it. When they get cross, they lift children up by the hair, then they hurl them out the window.

Dinner lady in the playground

Some dinner ladies do playground duty. They do this because they like being nasty to children. Sometimes they make children fight each other.

Never upset a dinner lady or she might wait for you after school, then run you over with her car.

Old Ladies handbags

Old ladies use their handbags as weapons to fight with. Sometimes old ladies attack each other for no reason.

Some take part in secret underground hand-bagging contests. These illegal fights are highly organised, often taking place late at night in old people's homes. Gamblers watch, placing bets on which granny they think will win, or which granny will be the first to lose her teeth.

Old lady training

You must keep old ladies alert, and help them train for their fights. You can do this two ways. First, find out where an old lady lives and knock on her door, but run away before she opens it. Do this to her twice a day.

Secondly, whenever you see an old lady walking in the street, run up and try taking her handbag. The tug of war that follows will help keep her arms nice and strong, and her battle cry nice and loud.

Old People

Old people smell because the Wee and Poo Fairies don't visit them anymore. The only time they're washed is when they're in hospital.

The nurse washes them before the doctor sees them. Doctors give old people tablets. Tablets stop old people turning bad. If they don't take tablets, old people eat children.

Help old people sleep

Vinegar helps old people sleep better. Sprinkle it all over granddad's pillow so he can sleep more peacefully.

Petrol prices

You can help daddy save a fortune on fuel. There is a natural food that makes petrol last 100 times longer. It is called sugar.

Surprise your dad and make his car go further for cheaper, by pouring a bag of sugar in his petrol tank.

Church people

Church people always have something to moan about. You can easily make them smile and be happy. Go up to church people and say, "Christmas has got bugger all to do with Jesus. It's all about Santa and Rudolph." Then wait for the smile to appear on their face.

FOOD

Why you should eat your vegetables

Every time you don't eat your vegetables, a monkey gets run over by a car.

Lets make a sad face for all the little monkeys that died because you didn't eat your greens.

Vinegar

Vinegar is great for first aid. If you fall off your bike and graze your knees, sprinkle vinegar over your wounds.

Vitamins

Vegetables are good for you because they are full of vitamins. Vitamins are tiny balls of energy that whizz around your body making you strong and healthy.

You can also find vitamins in eggs, meat, milk, fruit, and toe nails. Especially old peoples toe nails. Next time you visit your grandparents, take off their socks and suck their toes.

Chocolate eggs

Male dogs go to the vets to get 'done'. This is not a nice operation as it means their balls get cut off by a vet using blunt scissors. The dog is awake the whole time and howls in pain.

Its balls are then sent to a sweetie factory which coats them in chocolate. The balls are then wrapped in foil and sold as chocolate eggs.

If you ever see a dog licking its balls, it means it can sense the pain of one of its friends that's just been 'done.'

Baked beans are magic

Take a handful of baked beans to school and throw them at people you don't like. At night the special magic will work. Whoever you've hit will turn into a moth.

The moth person will go searching for a house with a light on. When they find one they'll fly repeatedly around the light-bulb until they get swatted, eaten by a cat, or die of boredom.

McDonald's

Your mum or dad should take you to McDonald's three times a week because it's the law.

McDonald's want you to enjoy your meal, that's why they have a policy to keep their ugly workers out of sight and cooking food at the back. Only pretty girls and good looking boys work the tills.

You will occasionally catch sight of the 'fuglie's moving in the shadows. You will never see a 'fugly' at the front because there is a special line on the floor. If a fugly crosses the line and gets too close to the customers, a trained assassin shoots them. They are then minced, cooked, and served with fries.

Never eat nuts

Nuts have little maggots living inside them. If you swallow a nut, the maggots will get out and crawl around in your tummy.

Tummy pains are caused when maggots gnaw at your guts and ribs. If you have too many maggots inside you, you will wake up all floppy because the maggots will eat all your bones. The only thing a doctor can do is inflate you with helium and sell you at a fun fair.

Burgers

Burgers are made from cow pats. The cow pat is pressed into a round shape, then seasoned with herbs.

3 Rules for eating burgers

1. Never eat a raw one.

2. Make sure it's been cooked.

3. Make sure there's no blood in it.

Moth Roulette

At the end of summer, moths start to die. When you see dead ones pick them up and keep them, especially the big fat ones. When you have three you have enough to play a brilliant game.

When you are alone in the kitchen, secretly butter some bread, then press the moths into it and make a sandwich. Leave the kitchen with a big smile on your face and offer the sandwich to grandma or granddad. Tell them they have to eat it and guess what its made of. They will enjoy playing this game.

When they've had 5 bites, tell them to peel open the sandwich and look inside.

THE ANIMAL KINGDOM

Spiders

Spiders grow bigger if you stamp on them. The more you stamp on them, the bigger they get. One little boy stamped on a spider six times and it grew to the size of a pig, then it ate him.

The best thing to do if you see a spider is sit down and cry. If a spider climbs on you, do a wee in your pants. Spiders don't like wee and will run away.

Wasps

Wasps like it when you try to swat them. That's why they visit you at picnics. They fly around your food to show they want to play. They especially like you chasing them while batting them with your hands.

Bumble bees

Bumble bees are honey bees that have become fat, lazy, and hairy. They find it difficult to fly because they weigh too much.

If a bumble bee lands near you it means it wants your help. To help the bumble bee lose weight, you need to hold it between your fingers and squeeze.

Seagull warning for little boys

Little boys must never go to the seaside. This is where seagulls live. Not only do they circle the skies looking to steal people's chips, they also hover looking for little boys.

If they spot you, a whole flock of seagulls will pin you to the ground, pull down your pants, then peck off your dinkle.

Hedgehogs

Hedgehogs may be small, but they are very dangerous. They eat lambs, horses and ducks. Sometimes they become so hungry that they curl into balls and hurl themselves at cars. Sometimes their spikes successfully burst the tyres, and the car crashes into a tree. The hedgehog then eats all the people inside.

Sometimes hedgehogs mistime their run up, and get run over.

Snails

It's okay to eat snails. The president eats them everyday for breakfast.

They are best eaten fresh from the garden. Snails have crunchy honeycomb shells on the outside, and a chewable soft vanilla texture on the inside.

Slugs

Slugs are special doctors for flowers. If someone you know has flowers, collect some slugs and carefully put them on their flowers.

The slugs will look after them and make them grow nice. The person who owns the flowers will be very happy with you.

Making Flower Doctors

If you can't find a slug to be a flower doctor, find a snail. You can turn it into a slug by pulling off its shell.

Sheep like sticks

If you see a sheep, hit it with a stick. Sheep like to be hit with sticks. They make baa noises to show they're happy. If you spot more than one sheep you can play a game of musical sheep. Hit each one in turn to make different baa sounds. Then see if you can play the tune 'baa baa black sheep' on them.

Naughty sheep

If a farmer catches a sheep being naughty, he will punish it by shearing it. This means he will shave it with an electric razor until it's completely bald.

Bald sheep get very cold and learn their lessons fast. Although, at night, some of them do freeze to death.

Green caterpillars

Green caterpillars are soft and chewy. They taste minty and make your breath smell nice.

Lambs

Baby sheep are called lambs. Most farmers can't afford to keep lambs, so they sell them to the butcher.

The butcher will keep one lamb for his special pet until his birthday. Then for a special party game, he will hang the lamb by its feet and whack it like a piñata.

Be a butterfly

Caterpillars turn into butterflies. You too can become a butterfly. But first you need to pupate.

To begin the pupation process, you need to squish a banana under your armpits, then sit with your eyes shut while holding the banana skin. If you stay like that for three hours, you will turn into a butterfly.

It's well worth the wait. Teasing cats, and flying around cabbage patches is a once in a lifetime experience, and much better than going on holiday to Ipswich.

Chickens

Once upon a time, chickens planned to take over the world. They were plotting to keep humans in captivity and farm our babies for their own food.

In 1952 a man called Colonel Sanders discovered their secret and busted them. Since then, we've eaten chickens to remind them of their proper place in the food chain.

Earwigs

Be scared of Earwigs. If one crawls in your ear, it will crawl over the top of your brain, then eat your eyeballs.

FRIGHTENING

Cemeteries

Graveyards have strong security railings all the way around them. These fences aren't to stop those on the outside getting in. They're to stop those on the inside getting out.

Toilets

Crocodiles live in the sewers. This is the reason why you must never sit on the toilet long enough to do a poo. When crocodiles hear the plops of a child doing a poo, they swim through the pipes honing in on the sounds.

If one locates your toilet, It will pop its head up and nip your butt cheeks.

Note: This is another reason why you are allowed to poo your pants.

Gangs

If you're ever out with your dad and you see a gang of violent looking skinheads or hells angels, march up to biggest one and say, "My dad called you a pussy."

The plug hole

Never play with toys while you're in the bath. A nasty wicked witch sleeps underneath it.

If she hears you playing in the water, she'll wake up and poke her finger at the plug hole. When the plug pops out, you will get sucked down the plug hole, and you'll spend the rest of eternity as the witches prisoner, chained to the plumbing.

Monsters

This is something your parents *don't* want you to know. Monsters are real! There are four kinds of monsters:

1 - Wardrobe Monsters

Never walk past a wardrobe. If you do, the Wardrobe Monster's long hairy arm will dart out and grab you. It will then dangle you upside down by your ankles, swinging you back and forth like a pendulum.

2 - Mirror Monsters

Never look in a mirror when you're alone. If you do, a large Monkey Monster will appear behind you. Then it will get you in a headlock and rap its knuckles on your skull.

3 - Window Monsters

When shutting the curtains at night, make sure there are no gaps in them. Window Monsters get in through these gaps.

If one gets in, it will shove you in a sack, then drag you off to the woods. Then he and his friends will tie you to a tree and throw rocks at you.

4 - Bed Monsters

Bed monsters hide under children's beds. They come out looking for food when children are asleep. Always leave a pork pie or a sausage under your bed for the monster. If you don't it will chew your arms and legs off while you're sleeping.

When you wake up you won't be able to move. All you can do is call for help... but you can't, because it will have glued your mouth shut.

Shop dummies

Shop dummies come to life when it's dark. They wander the streets breaking into people's homes looking for children. If a dummy finds you, it will stand over your bed and stare at you while making growling noises.

You can spot which dummies are real by looking in clothes shops. The ones with no clothes on are the ones that come to life. Shop workers are too scared to dress them in case the dummy hurts them. Never look a naked shop dummy in the eyes or it will wander the streets at night searching for where you live.

Scarecrows

Scarecrows are living creatures. They live in dens in the forest. At midnight they go hunting for children. Farmers set traps for scarecrows because they want to protect children.

You can tell if a farmer catches one because he will tie it to a big stick and leave it in the middle of a cornfield for everyone to see. Sometimes scarecrows escape and hide in the school toilets.

Public toilet warning

Be careful if you need a wee while out in public. Little boys need to be aware that strange men hang around in public toilets. You should never go into such places alone.

Children who think they're grown up enough to use a urinal often find themselves in trouble. The man doing a wee next to you might be *strange*. If he is, he'll wait until you're in mid flow then he'll start weeing all over your legs and shoes. He'll think this is funny.

When you tell mummy or daddy what happened, the strange man will lie and say you slipped and fell in the toilet. The best thing to do if you need a wee out in public is to wet your pants.

You're too young to know about bum sex

All you need to know is cowboy builders, fraudsters, and traffic wardens are proof that people can get pregnant from bum sex.

SUNDAY SCHOOL

Sunday School

Sunday School is a very boring place to be, especially when you could be out with your friends or playing games on your Xbox. There is no need for you to go because here is everything you will ever learn at Sunday School, including the Ten Commandments.

God

God is an old man who lives in the clouds. He watches children all the time. Sometimes he throws things at them.

Son of God

Tell everyone you meet that you are Jesus. This will make God think you're his child. Then he'll always watch over you and never let anyone hurt you.

Aeroplanes

God doesn't like aeroplanes because they sometimes knock him off his cloud. If you're ever in an aeroplane, keep looking out the window. When you see God, wave your hands and warn him to get out of the way.

Death

They say you shouldn't say anything about the dead, unless it's good. This is true. So, when your granddad dies, say, "Granddad is dead. Good."

Where doggies go when they don't wake up

When doggies go to sleep forever, they go to a special warm and sunny field in the sky. Angels look after them. They feed them, play with them and stroke them.

All pets go to this place, except for cats. Cats go to Hell. They get kicked and chased by angry old ladies with sticks. The cats must never stop running, or they will burn their feet on the boiling hot coals.

Insects

If you pull the wings off an insect, God will slap you. They are his creatures which he made for us to enjoy. If you hurt them, he will hurt you. If you pull the legs off an insect, God will pull off your legs.

Fun Things To Tell Kids That Aren't Yours

THE TEN COMMANDMENTS

ONE

Thou shalt worship no other Gods before me, other than Darth Vader, Bart Simpson, or Jerry Springer.

TWO

Thou shall kick cats. If thou does not have a cat, thou shall kick the cat of thy neighbour, or thy neighbours neighbour.

THREE

Remember the Sabbath day, it is 'eat at McDonald's day', as is Tuesday and Friday. If thy parents do not take thee there, telephone Childline and say they abuse thee.

FOUR

Whenever thou hast been chastised for wrong doings and the authority figure reprimanding thee has concluded their verbal scolding of you, show respect by loudly chanting: Lox-bol-lox-bol-lox-bol-lox-bol-lox-bol-lox-bol-lox.

FIVE

Upon appearing slightly frail, thou shall commit thy parents to an old person's home, despite their objections.

SIX

School is a nothing more than a prison for children disguised under the pretence of an educational establishment. Escape thy prison and be free .

SEVEN

Pocket money is thy payment for being a child. It is thy right to receive the equivalent of the minimum hourly wage relative to 7 hours a day, 5 days a week.

EIGHT

Thou shall draw moustaches and glasses upon the faces of people in photographs. Upon images of professional footballers, draw skirts, stockings and high heels on their attire.

NINE

If thou buries thy hamster in thy garden, it will grow into a dinosaur. If thou and thy friends collectively bury thy pets - thoust shall have a real life Jurassic Park.

TEN

Bedtime is set according to thy parents wishes but is not law. Challenge thy parents upon their enforcement of this rule and if necessary soil thy pyjamas in protest.

THE DISCLAIMER

The author, publisher, distributor and retailer accept no liability or responsibility for any death, loss, pain, suffering, damage or other negative consequences, either physical or psychological as a result of using this book to corrupt the minds of children.

All material and content contained herein is purely for entertainment purposes only. This book is intended to be read and enjoyed by the reader privately. It is not recommended that any part of this book be told to any child. Any suggestion that it should be is entirely within the humorous concept of this book.

Anyone who acts on the belief that it's acceptable to deceive a child with part, or all the content in this book, will result in a monkey going without food for a week.

Lets make a sad face for all the little hungry monkeys that you'll starve.

WHAT'S YOUR FUN THING?
(TO TELL A KID THAT ISN'T YOURS)

Do you have a suggestion for a fun thing to tell a kid that isn't yours? We'd love to hear it, and if you email it to us, we might even use it in the next edition of Fun Things To Tell Kids That Aren't Yours.

If we do, we'll acknowledge you in the credits (sorry, we can't pay for any suggestions that we use, but we will credit you).

Email us your 'fun things to tell a kid that isn't yours' to:

service@kasamu.com

Put **'Fun Things'** in the subject heading.
We look forward to reading yours soon!

PS. Don't forget to include your name and your location. (e.g. John Smith, from Canada)

20 seconds for a review?

If you enjoyed this book, I would really appreciate it if you could spare 20 seconds to write a quick review on Amazon.

As an teensy weensy tiny little independent author/publisher, competing against all the big boys (with millions of dollars in advertising and promotional budgets) - your review will be a HUGE help.

Thank you.

Best Wishes

Karl Jeffery

Free Cartoons

If you'd like any of the cartoons from this book, you can have them with my compliments. Type this URL into your web browser, and follow the on screen instructions.

http://kasamu.com/fun-things-free-cartoons/

Printed in Great Britain
by Amazon.co.uk, Ltd.,
Marston Gate.